MORE CARD TRICKS

Written by
Gordon Hill

Copyright © 2005 Top That! Publishing plc.

Tangerine Press

an imprint of
SCHOLASTIC
www.scholastic.com

Scholastic and Tangerine Press and associated logos are trademarks of Scholastic Inc.
Published by Tangerine Press, an imprint of Scholastic Inc., 557 Broadway, New York, NY 10012
10 9 8 7 6 5 4 3 2 1
0-439-78525-1
Printed and bound in China

24 SEVEN Contents

You can have a blast creating magic; and there are thousands of different tricks that can be done with just a pack of cards.

Amaze and Entertain

Playing cards are reasonably cheap, and they don't take up much room. Carry a pack with you all the time and always be ready to amaze and entertain people with your fantastic magic!

Keep it Secret

In this book you will find lots of different tricks you can show your family and friends. Although you will learn the methods of magic, you should never tell anyone else what these are. Never give away the secret of a trick no matter how hard people ask. Practice in private, and don't let anyone watch your practice sessions.

Personality

Surprisingly enough, the methods by which a trick is achieved is not the most important part of magic. The most important part is the performer. A performer with a good personality and a winning smile is much more important that exactly how the trick is done. So always smile and enjoy your magic; this is important if you want to be successful.

Enjoy Yourself!

Magic is a fascinating hobby and is great fun. So, whether you just want to show a few tricks to small groups or to become an international magician, there is no better way to start than with a pack of cards.

Mix up the cards with an overhand shuffle. All card players use this simple shuffling technique.

The overhand shuffle is the most common way to mix up a pack of cards so nobody knows what order they are in. To do card magic, you must be able to do a good overhand shuffle; but it is fairly easy to learn. Just keep practicing until you can do it well.

1. Hold the pack in your left hand with the thumb supporting it on the left side, the forefinger at the end, and the other three fingers on the face of the bottom card.

2. Bring the right hand over and pick up the bottom three quarters of the pack.

3. Drop a few of the cards from the right hand onto the top of the pack, and then lift your right hand away.

4. Drop a few more cards on the top of the pack from the right hand, and keep repeating these movements until all the cards are back in the left hand.

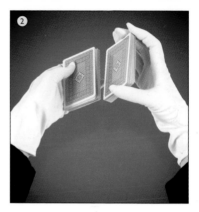

5. Keep practicing until you can do it quickly. If you are left handed, you may find it easier to hold the pack in the right hand and shuffle off with the left.

How to shuffle the cards while keeping certain cards on the top of the pack.

3. Continue shuffling in the normal way until you end up with one card sticking out of the pack.

I. To practice this, first put the four aces on the top of the pack.

2. Start a normal overhand shuffle, but drop one card only on the first movement. Drop this card so it protrudes over the end of the cards in the left hand.

4. Bring the right hand to the pack so that your thumb tip touches the protruding card.

5. Take all the cards beneath the protruding card and put them on top of the pack, and at the same time push the protruding card flush with the rest of the cards.

6. You appear to have given a real shuffle, but the four aces will still be on the top!

Special Tip

When you try this shuffle for the first time, allow the protruding card to stick out quite a lot. This means that it is difficult to hide from the audience. With practice, you should be able to reduce the amount of "sticking out" to almost nothing so the audience will not see or suspect anything crafty.

The aces are such good friends they always group together.

1. Take the four aces and two other cards from the pack.

4. Put the next two cards in different parts of the pack. You do not show these cards, but the audience will assume they are aces.

2. Show the four aces, but keep the two extra cards hidden under the third ace. Then put the cards on the top of the pack.

3. Take the top card, show that it is an ace, and put it on the bottom of the pack.

5. Lift off the top half of the pack and place it on the bottom. Tell your audience that the aces are such good friends that they do not like being separated. Spread the cards face up and show that the aces have come together in the middle of the pack.

An easy way to find a card chosen by a spectator.

1. Secretly arrange the pack so that each suit is in numerical order.

2. When you want to show the trick, ask someone to take any card from the pack, remember it and then put it back in a different position.

3. All you have to do is look through the pack and take out the card that is not in the correct place.

4. Show it to the audience — it is the chosen card!

Special Tip

It is a good idea to get the spectator to show the chosen card to the rest of the audience. People can easily forget which card they chose, so if this happens the audience can remind them.

Cards are mixed up, but they stay in the same order. You will amaze yourself with this trick!

1. Take ten cards, ace to ten, and arrange them in numerical order. Turn the cards face-down and say you are going to deal the cards onto the table.

2. You deal one card at a time unless the spectator says "down under." When that happens, take the card you are about to deal, place it under the next card, and put both cards down together.

3. Continue to deal through the packet like this, dealing one card at a time except when the spectator calls out "down under" – which can be at any time.

4. When all ten cards are on the table, pick them up and say "Let's do that again to make sure they are well mixed."

5. Again, deal the cards as you did before with the spectator calling out "down under" at any time. Now spread out the ten cards face-up – they are still in their original order from one to ten!

Magic words are used to find a card that someone is only thinking of.

1. Deal three piles of seven cards. Spread out the cards in each pile and ask a spectator to think of any card and tell you which pile it is in.

2. Put the three piles together, with the chosen pile between the other two. Deal the cards into three piles once again.

3. Spread the cards out face-up and ask which pile now contains the "thought-of" card. Put the three piles together, again with the chosen pile going between the others.

4. Repeat step 3.

5. Now deal the cards onto the table, one at a time to spell out the words "that's magic," one card going down for each letter. Ask the spectator to name the card being thought of. Turn over the next card – it is the chosen card! Now that's magic!

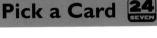

You find a card that has been chosen and returned to the pack.

1. Ask someone to shuffle the cards.

2. Take the pack and give it one cut. As you do this, secretly glimpse at the bottom card of the pack and remember it. This is your "key" card.

3. Spread out the cards face-down and ask a spectator to take any card, remember it, and then put it back on the top of the pack.

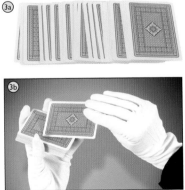

4. Cut the pack to lose the chosen card somewhere in the middle. This actually puts your "key" card next to the chosen card.

5. Spread the cards before your eyes and look for your key card. The chosen card is the one to the right of your key.

6. Take out the chosen card and ask the spectator what card was chosen. When the card is named, turn it over and enjoy the applause.

The royal families get mixed up and then sort themselves out again.

1. Take the king, queen, jack and ace of spades and lay them out in a row on the table. Say "One day the Spade royal family decided to hold a party."

2. "They invited the Heart royal family, the king, the queen, the prince and the princess (ace)." Place each of these on top of the cards on the table as you talk.

3. "And the king, queen, prince and princess of clubs." Put each of the club cards on top of those on the table.

4. "They even invited the Royal House of Diamonds to the party." Put the king, queen, jack and ace of diamonds on top of the others.

5. Put the four piles together, one on top of the other, and then turn them face-down. "And they danced the night away." As you say this, keep cutting the pile of cards to give the impression that they are being well mixed (do not shuffle them).

6. Now deal the cards out into four face-down piles as you say "At the end of the evening, the carriages arrived and the royal families each went home to their own palace." Turn each pile over in turn and spread them out on the table to show that each of the four suits have grouped themselves together.

7. "The Diamond family went home to their palace, the Clubs to theirs, the Hearts to theirs and the Spades went to bed." Pick up all the cards and put them back into the box.

Four ordinary cards and a queen are placed in envelopes. Even though the envelopes are mixed up, you can tell which one contains the queen.

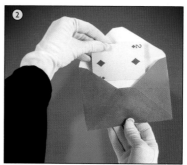

1. Show five empty envelopes and five playing cards, one of which is a queen. Ask a spectator to hand you an envelope and one of the cards.

2. Place the card in the envelope and drop the envelope on the table. Do exactly the same with the other envelopes and cards.

3. What the spectators do not know is the cards are placed in the envelopes horizontally (on their sides) but when the queen is placed in an envelope, it is secretly turned as soon as it is out of sight so it stands vertically (upright).

4. Mix the envelopes and hold them behind your back. Feel each envelope and find which one holds the queen. Because it is positioned differently from the other cards, it is easy to find.

5. Bring the queen envelope forward, reach into it and turn the queen to a horizontal position before taking it out of the envelope.

The cards tell you how many cards have been moved while your back is turned.

1. Arrange ten cards, numbered from ace to ten, in numerical order. Your audience must not know about this secret preparation.

3. Say you are going to turn your back and you want someone to move any number of cards up to nine, one at a time, from the left end of the row to the right end.

4. You show what you mean by taking three cards from the left to the right end.

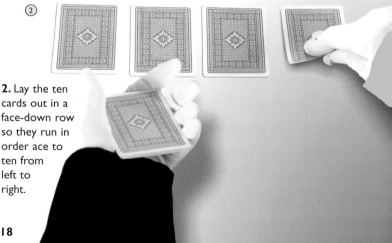

2. Lay the ten cards out in a face-down row so they run in order ace to ten from left to right.

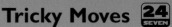
5. Turn away and get someone to move some cards.

6. When this has been done, turn back again and mentally count three cards from the right end of the row and turn over the fourth. That card will tell you how many cards have been moved. If, for example, three cards were moved then the card you turn over will also be a three.

7. You can do the trick again, but this time you add together the number of cards that have already been moved.

8. The trick can even be repeated a third time provided that you again total the number of cards that have been moved.

9. If the card turned over is a ten, it means that the spectator has tried to trick you and that no cards have been moved.

You look into the future and name three cards before they are picked from the pack.

1. While talking to the audience, secretly look at the bottom card of the pack. Remember the card (let's say it is the 6 of clubs).

2. Say you are now going to have three cards chosen. Ask someone to take the top card from the pack and place it face-down on the table.

3. As this is being done say, "I think that will be the 6 of clubs." (The card you remembered.)

4. Pick up the chosen card and look at it (but do not show it to the audience). Let us assume that this card is the eight of diamonds. Just say "good" and put the card back on the table.

5. Ask a second spectator to pull the eight of diamonds (the card you have just seen) from the center of the pack and place it face down on top of the first card.

6. Again, pick up the card and say something like, "I think I'm getting good at this." Let us assume that this card is the queen of hearts.

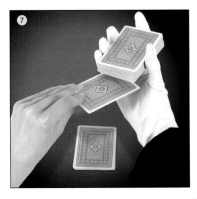

7. Get a third spectator to pull the queen of hearts from the bottom of the pack and, without looking at it, place it on top of the other two cards.

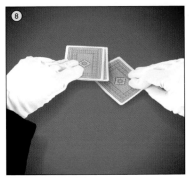

8. Pick up the last chosen card (actually the first card you remembered) and say, "That's amazing!" Look at the audience as you say this and slide the card in your hand under the other two cards to turn them over. All three cards are seen to be the actual ones you named in advance!

Read a spectator's mind and call it magic!

1. Ask someone to shuffle the cards, then place the pack on the table and cut into two equal piles.

3. Ask the spectator to pick up one of the piles, take out one card, remember it, show it to the rest of the audience, then put it on top of the pile.

2. Push the piles side by side and ask the spectator to move cards from one pile to the other so each pile is exactly the same (or as near as possible).

4. Get the spectator to re-assemble the pack by putting the other pile on top of the chosen card so it is lost somewhere in the middle of the pack.

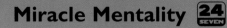

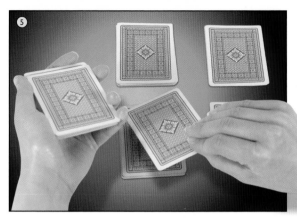

5. The spectator is now asked to deal out four piles of cards using all of the pack.

6. Pick up each pile in turn, spread it out in front of the spectator and ask if the chosen card is in that pile. Discard the three piles that do not contain the chosen card.

7. You now look at the cards you hold and read the spectator's mind by announcing the name of the chosen card.

8. How did you do it? Simple! The chosen card will be the middle card of the ones you are holding. Try to sound mysteriously magical when you announce the name of the chosen card.

23

A magic clock reveals the identity of a chosen card.

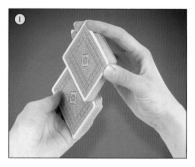

1. Ask someone to shuffle the cards and then hand the pack back to you.

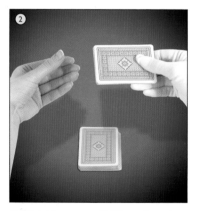

2. Quickly count off 13 cards and hand them to a spectator. Do not say anything about the number of cards in this packet. Put the rest of the pack on the table.

3. Turn away as you say that you want the spectator to take any number of cards from the small packet and put them in a pocket or sit on them.

4. The rest of the cards are then to be shuffled and one card chosen. This card must be remembered, placed on the bottom of the packet and the packet then put back on top of the pack.

5. You now turn back to face the audience as you say you are going to use the cards to make a clock face. Deal 12 cards into the positions of the numbers on a clock, starting at 12 o'clock and then moving around in an anti-clockwise direction. This means that the second card goes at the 11 o'clock position, the third at ten o'clock and so on around the clock face.

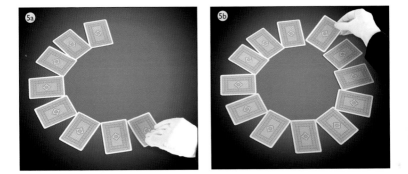

6. Ask the spectator to count how many cards were removed from the packet at the start of the trick. You then count to that position on the clock face – so, if five cards were taken, you count to five o'clock, if eight cards were taken, you go to eight o'clock, and so on.

7. Ask for the name of the card that was chosen and turn over the card where you stopped counting in step 6.

8. It is the chosen card!

A chosen card is sandwiched between two other cards!

1. Have the pack shuffled. Cut the cards and secretly look at the bottom card. This is your "key" card – say its the 8 of hearts.

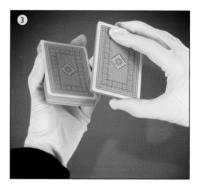

3. Cut the pack to lose the chosen card and then say that you are going to look through the pack for two slices of bread. This should make your audience laugh.

2. Ask a spectator to take a card, remember it and place it back on the top of the pack.

4. Say that you haven't really got two slices of bread in the pack so you will use two kings instead. Look through the cards for two kings, but at the same time look for your key card.

5. Take out the kings and then cut the cards to bring the key card to the bottom and the chosen card (next to it) to the top of the pack.

6. Hold the pack behind your back. Take one of the kings behind your back, turn it over and push it under the top card. Then take the other king behind your back, turn it over and place it on top of the pack (on top of the chosen card).

7. Cut the pack to move the two kings and the chosen card to the middle.

8. Bring the pack forward and spread it out on the table. The spectators will see the two face-up cards with another card between them.

9. Ask for the name of the chosen card and get someone to take the sandwiched card. It is the chosen card!

27

You look into the future and predict the name of a card that will be chosen.

1. Ask someone to shuffle the pack.

2. Take the cards back and spread their faces toward you very quickly as you say, "Yes, they look well-mixed."

3. What you are really doing is looking for the ninth card from the top of the pack. You must remember this card and you must practice so you can see this card quickly without

anyone realizing that you are counting up to nine.

4. Put the pack on the table and write down on a piece of paper the card you remembered at the ninth position. Do not let anyone see what you have written, but fold the paper and put it next to the pack of cards.

5. Ask someone to call out any number from ten to 19 and then to deal that number of cards from the top of the pack onto the table.

6. Now, ask for the digits of the chosen number to be added together and that number of cards removed from the cards just dealt. So, if the chosen number was 17, there would be eight cards (1 + 7) removed; if the number was 13, then four cards would be removed.

7. Turn over the next card of the packet and ask someone to read out what you wrote earlier. You will have predicted that very same card.

29

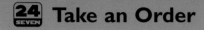
How to arrange a pack of cards in a secret order that can be useful in lots of card tricks.

There are many tricks that can be done in which the cards are in a set order known only to the magician. This type of arrangement is known as a stacked pack. A popular stack used by magicians all over the world is called the Si Stebbins, after the American performer who invented it.

1. Each card in the stack has a value three higher than the one before. So, a 4 is followed by a 7, which comes before 10, and so on. A jack is counted as 11, a queen is 12 and the value of a king is 13.

②

2. The order, from an ace is A, 4, 7, 10, K, 3, 6, 9, Q, 2, 5, 8, J.

3. The suits are also in order – clubs, hearts, spades, diamonds.

---

4. The complete pack, starting with an ace, looks like this:

AC, 4H, 7S, 10D, KC, 3H, 6S, 9D, QC, 2H, 5S, 8D, JC,

AH, 4S, 7D, 10C, KH, 3S, 6D, 9C, QH, 2S, 5D, 8C, JH,

AS, 4D, 7C, 10H, KS, 3D, 6C, 9H, QS, 2D, 5C, 8H, JS,

AD, 4C, 7H, 10S, KD, 3C, 6H, 9S, QD, 2C, 5H, 8S, JD.

Learn the System

1. Pick up the complete pack and cut it a few times. It looks as if the cards are getting mixed up; but cutting the cards does not change the order. The sequence just starts at a different card.

Special Tip

To learn the order of the suits, remember the word "chased." This gives you the order **CHaSeD** (clubs, hearts, spades, diamonds).

2. Cut the cards one more time and look at the bottom card. From that you can work out what card is on the top of the pack. It will be the next one in the sequence. So, if the bottom card is the 7 of diamonds, for example, the top card will be the 10 of clubs (add 3 to the 7 and go to the next suit in order). If the bottom card is the queen of spades, the top card will be the 2 of diamonds.

3. Keep practicing in this way until you can work out what is the top card. When you can do that quickly and accurately, turn to page 32 and start learning some of the fantastic tricks you can do with a Si Stebbins stack.

Special Tip

If you do any tricks in which a card is taken out of the pack, make sure it goes back in the same position or the sequence will be broken.

You prove that you have the amazing ability to see through your fingertips!

1. You need a pack of cards set up in the special arrangement described on page 30.

2. Spread the cards out face-down and invite someone to take any card, and, without looking at it, place it face-down in your right hand.

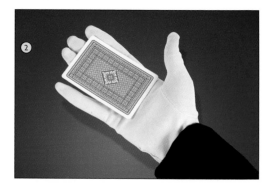

3. As you are telling the spectator what to do, cut the cards at the point where the card was removed and take a quick glimpse at the bottom card as you put the pack together.

4. Using the system, calculate what card the spectator has placed in your hand; pretend that you can see through your fingertips. Name the card and show everyone you are right.

5. Put the chosen card back on the pack, and you are ready to do the trick again. Do not repeat the trick more than three times or someone may figure you out.

You read the mind of a friend over the telephone!

1. Before calling a friend, write the numbers 1 to 26 on a sheet of paper.

2. Call a friend and ask him or her to get a pack of playing cards.

3. You now ask your friend to follow your instructions: "Shuffle the cards and then cut them into two roughly equal piles."

4. "Pick up one pile and push the other one to one side."

5. "Now count the number of cards in your chosen pile, but do it quietly so I can't hear."

6. "Have you done that? Good. Now, whatever number you have, add together the two digits of that number. If, for example, you have 21 cards, add the 2 and the 1 to get 3."

7. "Take that number of cards from your chosen pile and discard them."

8. "Now think of any number between one and ten. Take that number of cards from your pile and put them in your pocket. Again, do it so I cannot hear how many you have taken."

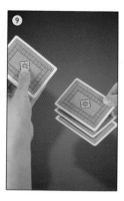

9. "Next, I want you to count down the same number of cards in what is left of your pile and memorize the card at that position."

10. "I think you will agree with me that there is no way I can know how many cards you have in your pocket or what card you are thinking of. So, I want you to do just one more thing."

11. "I want you to pick up your chosen pile and deal the remaining cards out one at a time calling out their names as you do so."

12. As each card is named, write it down on your numbered list, starting with one and working your way down.

13. When your friend has finished, look at the number against the last card called – that is the number of cards in your friend's pile.

14. You now have to do a quick calculation. If the number of cards is less than 9, subtract the number from 9. If the number is between 9 and 17, subtract it from 18. And if there are more than 18, subtract the number from 27. The number you arrive at is the number on your list against the card your friend has chosen.

15. Let's say, for example, your list shows that there are 13 cards in your friend's pile. Subtract 13 from 18 and you get 5, so the fifth card's name is the chosen card.

16. You can now tell how many cards are in the pile, how many cards are in your friend's pocket, and, even more amazingly, the card that your friend is thinking of!

The joker tells you the name of a chosen card even though nobody else has seen it.

1. For this trick, you need a pack of cards arranged in the order given on page 30.

2. Spread out the cards face-up and take out the joker (if there is more than one in your pack, take that out before showing this trick).

3. Turn the cards face-down and spread the cards out for a spectator to take one. Ask the spectator to put the card out of sight, perhaps in a pocket, without anyone seeing it.

4. As the chosen card is being put away, cut the pack at the point where the card was taken. Take a quick glimpse at the bottom card after you have done this. Using the system described on page 30, you now know the value of the chosen card.

5. Pick up the joker and put it to your ear as you pretend that he is whispering to you, and then announce the name of the chosen card.

One card is seen to be reversed in the pack, and surprisingly, it matches a card chosen earlier!

1. You will need two packs of cards for this trick. Reverse any card in one pack and put the cards back into their box. Take the same card from the second pack, put it on top of the pack and put that pack back into its box. Put a small pencil mark on the box that contains the reversed card and you are ready to show the trick.

2. Place the packs on the table and say: "Please take one of these packs."

3. You continue talking without taking a break, but what you say depends upon which box the spectator takes. If the marked box is taken you say, "...And put it somewhere out of my reach." Then you pick up the other box and take out the cards.

4. If the unmarked box is taken, you say, " ...And take out the cards." As you speak, push the marked box as far as you can to one side.

5. When the cards have been taken from the unmarked box, say, "Will you please deal some cards, one on top of the other, onto the table?" After six or seven cards have been dealt say, "Stop dealing at any time you want."

6. When the spectator stops dealing, pick up the dealt cards and push them together neatly and place them on top of, but at right angles to, the rest of the pack.

7. Ask the spectator to take out the cards from the other (marked) box and spread them out face-up. Somewhere in the middle of the pack there will be one face-down card (the one you put here before the performance).

8. Ask the spectator to turn that card over as you pick up the dealt cards from the other pack and show the bottom card of the packet. Both cards are the same!

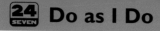
You and a spectator each choose a card – and by a magical coincidence you both pick the same one!

1. You will need two packs of cards. The spectator takes one pack and you have the other.

2. Ask the spectator to do exactly the same as you. Give your pack a shuffle and the spectator does the same.

3. You now exchange packs – but when handing your pack to the spectator, you take a secret glimpse at the bottom card. Remember that card.

4. From the pack that you now hold take out one card, look at it and put it on top of the pack. As the spectator does the same, say, "Remember your card." You do not have to remember the card you take.

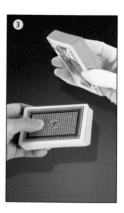

5. You both now cut the pack so the chosen card is lost somewhere in the middle.

6. Exchange packs once again. Ask the spectator to go through the pack, remove the chosen card, and place it face down on the table.

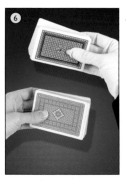

7. You appear to do the same; but what you really do is look for the card you secretly saw at the start of the trick. The card to the right of that card will be the one the spectator chose, and this is the one you remove and put face-down on the table.

8. Both cards are now turned over, and everyone is amazed to see that they are the same!

Two cards, chosen at random, come together in the pack.

1. Have the cards shuffled and cut into two piles. You take one pile and a spectator takes the other.

2. Ask the spectator to look through the cards in their half of the pack, take one out, remember it, place it on the top of the packet, and then put the packet on the table.

3. You appear to do exactly the same, but what you really do is look at and remember the card on the bottom of your packet. You take no notice whatsoever of the card you took from the pack.

42

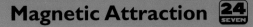

4. Put your packet of cards on top of the spectator's and then ask for the pack to be cut several times.

6. You name the card you saw on the bottom of the packet as your chosen card.

5. Now say that you will cause the two cards to come together in the pack. Ask the spectator for the name of his or her chosen card.

7. When the spectator looks through the pack, the two "chosen" cards will be together.

You predict what card will be found at the center point in the pack.

1. For this trick, you will need a pack of cards set in the order given on page 30.

2. Cut the pack several times. Do this quickly, and it will give the impression that the cards are being well mixed. Allow a spectator to cut the cards a few times as well.

3. Pick up the pack and secretly glimpse the bottom card. The 26th card from the top of the pack will be the same value as the bottom card and the other suit of the same color. So, if the bottom card is the ace of hearts, the 26th card will be the ace of diamonds.

4. Announce the name of the center card "even though you cannot possibly see it." A spectator deals down to the 26th card and confirms that it really is the card you named.

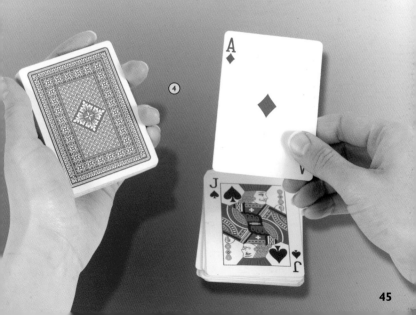

You show how the gamblers in Las Vegas can control the cards.

2. Deal out the first four cards as if dealing for a game of cards. Make sure the fourth card comes to you. Continue dealing into the four hands until each pile contains five cards.

1. You will need a pre-arranged pack of cards as on page 30 for this trick. Look for a 2 of any suit and cut the pack at that point as you turn all the cards face-down so the 2 is now on the bottom.

3. Pick up the first hand, the one to your left, and turn the cards face-up to show a complete sequence from the ace to the 5. A remarkable hand!

4. Pick up the second hand and this is a run from 4 to 8. Amazing! The third hand is a run from 7 to a jack. Fantastic!

5. But your hand is the best of the lot – a complete run from a 10 to an ace, which is known to gamblers as a royal flush. It must be magic!

Here you will find explanations for terms in the book that you may not be familiar with, and also some other terms that you might come across while playing cards.

Ace
Any of the four playing cards with only one spot.

Control
Keeping track of a card that has been chosen and returned to the pack.

Cut
Dividing the pack into two random parts after shuffling.

Deck
This is the same as "pack" and is a word used a lot by card magicians.

Effect
A description of what the trick looks like to the audience.

Fan
The shape in which dealt cards are usually held in the hand or the shape in which they are usually placed on the table.

Glimpse
Taking a secret look at one of the cards in the pack.

Index
The symbol in the corner that shows which card it is.

Joker
A card that does not belong to any suit, nor does it have a number. It can be used in some games and tricks, but is not always required.

Key Card
A card that helps the magician keep track of a chosen card.

Locator
Another name for a key card.

Overhand Shuffle
A basic shuffle.

Palm
Hiding a card in the hand.

Set-Up
A number of cards arranged in a special order before doing a trick.

Shuffle
Mixing up the pack to change the order of the cards.

Sleight
A crafty movement made by the magician's hand but isn't seen by the audience.

Stack
A number of cards arranged in a special order before doing a trick.

Suit
Any of four sets of 13 cards: clubs, diamonds, hearts or spades.